Food Grows in Soil

By Cameron Macintosh

T0342834

Contents

Food from Plants

Lots of food that we enjoy comes from plants.

Plants grow in soil.

Soil is a kind of dirt.

soil

First, we drop seeds into the soil.

To help the plants grow,
we must keep the soil moist.

Sun helps the plants grow, too.

seeds

soil

We can grow lots of kinds of plants in soil.

We can grow corn, kale and soy beans.

corn

kale

soy beans

You can chop up the kale
and roast it with oil.

Yum!

You can pick the soy beans and boil them.

Yum, yum!

We can enjoy grapes
that grow on vines in soil.

Even yummy plums grow
on trees in soil.

plums

grapes

Birds and Pests

Birds and other pests like to eat plants, too!

You can save your plants with tin foil.

ust tie some tin foil
on the plant.

Birds don't like tin foil
when it flaps!

They will fly off.

foil

Slugs and snails don't like foil.

They will stay off your plants.

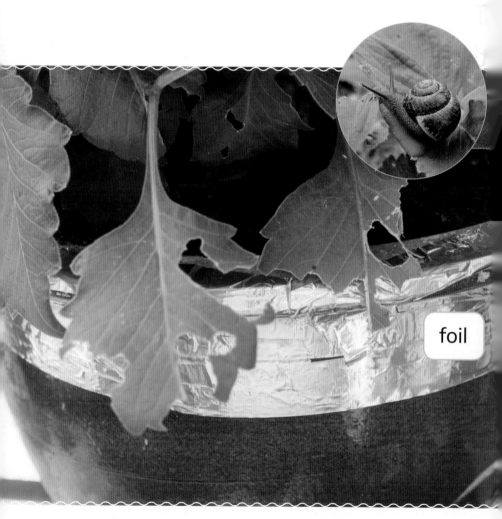

foil

You can put pointy sticks by your plants, too.

That will keep birds off the plants.

pointy sticks

This cowboy statue will give
the birds a shock, too!

Eat What You Grow

Lots of plants grow in soil.

Then we can enjoy eating them!

CHECKING FOR MEANING

1. What are some plants that can grow in soil? *(Literal)*

2. What can you tie on plants to keep birds and other pests off? *(Literal)*

3. How do you think pointy sticks will help keep birds off plants? *(Inferential)*

EXTENDING VOCABULARY

soil	What other word from the book has a similar meaning to *soil*? How would you describe soil?
moist	What is the meaning of the word *moist*? What other words do you know that have a similar meaning? E.g. wet, soggy.
cowboy	What two smaller words make up the word *cowboy*? How does this help you to work out what the word means?

MOVING BEYOND THE TEXT

1. What is your favourite plant that grows in soil?

2. What do plants need to be able to grow?

3. What are some different ways that you can cook food that comes from plants?

4. How else could you keep pests such as birds and insects away from plants?

DIPHTHONGS

| oy | ow | oo | aw |

PRACTICE WORDS

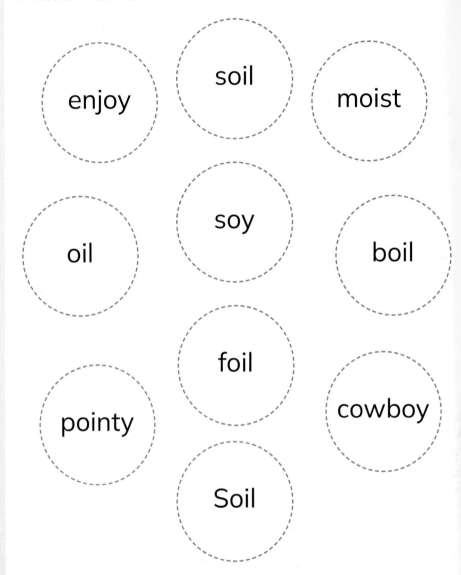

enjoy

soil

moist

oil

soy

boil

pointy

foil

cowboy

Soil